By Nina Roesner
Author of
The RESPECT Dare
(Thomas Nelson, 2012)

12 Truths to Change Your Marriage
(Greater Impact, 2014)

365 Ways to Love Your Wife
(Greater Impact, 2015)

With All Due Respect
(Thomas Nelson, 2016)

101 Ways to Respect Your Husband

Published by Greater Impact, 554 Belle Meade Farm Drive, Loveland, OH 45140

Disclaimer: The names and details surrounding many of the stories have been changed to protect the identity of individuals. Any association with specific individuals is purely unintended.

Printed in the United States of America.

Introduction

This little book is written in response to the many women who just want to know the answers to two questions:

- What does respect actually look like?
- How do I respect my husband?

This book is not meant to be a comprehensive study. It's merely a small background, a bit of explanation, and a list of 101 things you can actually DO that many men would consider respectful. This is a conversational summary of research and Biblical information. If you want the details of either, please check *12 Truths to Change Your Marriage,* (Greater Impact, August 14, 2014) or *The Respect Dare: 40 Days to a Deeper Relationship with God & Your Husband* (Thomas Nelson, 2012)

You will also find that I mention some of our training programs and the books I've written. Please know it is not my intent to be promotional, however, I can't help talking about them because that's where the list comes from – women in these classes whose lives have been changed by applying many things, but also the points on the list. Please forgive me if I come across as "sales-ish" in any way. I am not a professional author, as you've probably figured out by now already, but rather a trainer.

Honestly, if you participate in anything from Greater Impact, I hope you enroll in our FREE Strength & Dignity eCourse. It's for women who are at risk of becoming "doormats" in their marriages. I'll talk about that some before we get started with the list because there's one thing you need to understand:

*Your respect will **only** be perceived as valuable to your husband if you are a wife who respects herself.*

That may sound counter-intuitive to you, but it is vitally important that you understand this concept.

Think about it like this – for sake of analogy, we'll use a running goal to help make the point. If you are a runner, and you want to increase your distance to the point that you can not only run a marathon, but run one of the most prestigious marathons in the country, The Boston Marathon®, you will need to learn how to do that. Maybe you are blessed in that you live in a neighborhood with a lot of runners. Maybe one of those runners has not only run several marathons over the years, but she's also qualified for Boston. Maybe she even placed first in her age division. We'll call her Rayna. You know all this about her because you've seen her running at 6:00am and you read the details about her Boston experience in the local newspaper.

Maybe one of your other neighbors is a weekend warrior. Every Saturday, around 10:00am, you see your next door neighbor out there jogging. We'll call her Wendy. Wendy doesn't run any other day during the week, and she's never done a race. You know these things because you talk over the fence now and again.

Which woman are you going to talk to? Rayna the Boston marathoner or Wendy the weekend warrior?

That's easy, right?

Here's how it applies to respect.

The power and value of respect comes down to one thing: *credibility*. If you go run a 5K and tell either women about your experience and your time, and both of them say, "Wow! That's a pretty good time! You'll be running Boston in no time!" ... *which one do you believe?*

Which woman's comment has more credibility?

Rayna's of course!

So if you are a wife who treats herself with respect (and that's what the Strength & Dignity eCourse is about) and then shows respect to her husband, she is going to have *credibility*. He's going to believe her because he's receiving admiration and honor from a princess.

If you are a wife who consistently disrespects herself by throwing herself under the bus physically, emotionally, mentally, wearing herself out in the name of "serving others," and being taken advantage of, your respect means little because you treat yourself as a peasant.

Whose respect means more to a man? Respect from the daughter of a King, or a peasant?

Coming up, you'll see a short quiz to determine whether or not you demonstrate behaviors that put you in either category. And don't worry – we're NOT endorsing selfishness! We're also NOT suggesting that wives STOP serving their husband and kids! But we have to see there is a balance. In our Western culture, you'll see that we typically engage in something I refer to as "pendulum swinging." We've had this concept in all of our training classes since we started in 2005.

Essentially it involves finding the happy, holy, healthy "middle ground" and avoiding extremist "black and white thinking," which psychologists and educators will tell us is detrimental to mental health and relationships. Too many people in our culture do not understand real Win-Win relationships – they only understand Win-Lose or Lose-Win. In other words, if someone wins, the other has to be losing, right?

Wrong.

Just recently, I watched a dialogue unfold online where someone said she enjoyed serving her husband. What followed suit blew me away. Several women chimed in with "just because he has a penis," and "he has to earn it," and "he has no right to be served just because he is a man" comments. Sorry for the graphic truth there – but do you see how a sweet woman's thought set off a whole lot of defensive behavior? These women swung to the side of the pendulum that assumes that a woman who feels good about serving her husband has to be a doormat, right? What they didn't know is that the woman was actually respected by her husband – and he served her, too, but that wasn't what she was feeling all sweet about at the moment. The unfortunately thing is that too often, these criticizers swing to the "domineering" side of the pendulum – where the only place a woman has value, in their minds, is if SHE is in CONTROL.

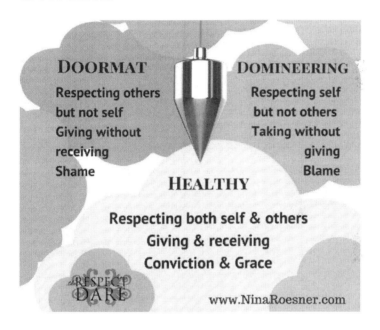

DOORMAT

Respecting others but not self

Giving without receiving

Shame

DOMINEERING

Respecting self but not others

Taking without giving

Blame

HEALTHY

Respecting both self & others

Giving & receiving

Conviction & Grace

RESPECT DARE

www.NinaRoesner.com

It's true that there are both types of women (and men) like that out there. Individuals who are easily taken advantage of become doormats. Individuals who fight against others and have to have all the power are domineering.

We believe that what God wants is in the middle.

Healthy. Holy. And the end result? Happy.

So before I launch into the list of 101 Ways to Respect Your Husband, I'm going to ask you to take a moment and discern whether you are a Daughter of a King (desired) or a peasant (not desired). Glance through the following, putting check marks next to what applies:

Daughter of a King:

- ○ Serves out of love, not obligation
- ○ Rests when she cannot serve or her service suffers because she is depleted
- ○ Speaks the truth in love, even if others will not approve or agree
- ○ Says what she means instead of saying what the other person wants to hear
- ○ Isn't "punitive" or "parental" in her responses when others cross her boundaries, but rather can calmly communicate her response (for example, "I want to talk about this, but can't right now. Let's talk later when we're both calm" – leaves the room).
- ○ Serves out of obedience to God, not out of obligation or fear of others' opinions
- ○ Cares for others AND is also cared for BY others (whether out of love, need, or want)
- ○ Speaks kindly and respectfully to others, AND others speak kindly and respectfully to her – not out of fear on either side
- ○ Is comfortable saying, "No," to requests when they are not things God wants her to do
- ○ Has empathy and compassion for others' being disappointed in her "No," but does not feel guilt or shame over someone else's disappointment
- ○ She gives AND receives freely from others without expectation of obligations
- ○ She takes responsibility for her decisions, mistakes, etc., but does not own the reactions of others, extending grace and compassion to herself

- She follows her convictions, respecting her own thoughts, ideas, wants, and needs, without making excuses or condemning herself – while allowing others to do the same without condemning them
- She knows and accepts her strengths and weaknesses
- She creates and executes healthy boundaries for herself like, "I will not react when I am emotional, but respond when I have self-control," and, "I'll only eat dessert on days that I exercise," etc.
- Takes time to be with friends and engage in activities that are important to her – even if no one else in her family is interested
- Respects others, serves, sacrifices, but also takes care of herself
- She asks for help when she needs it and freely offers her help when asked by others

Peasant

- Changes her plans to keep the peace
- Consistently does more work than others in similar circumstances
- Fails to rest when she is tired
- Apologizes for things she didn't do just to make someone else happy
- Puts other people's wants and needs above her own such that her own desires are seldom, if ever, known about or acted upon by others
- Consistently changes what she enjoys doing to meet the desires of others – to the point of taking up their hobbies and interests without pursuing her own
- Consistently gives up dreams she's had since childhood

- Consistently sacrifices her health, time, energy, or money to help rescue people from poor decisions or outcomes
- Consistently makes excuses for other people's lack of care or proper attention to her or her children
- Consistently stays silent to avoid upsetting someone else when her feelings are hurt, lies are told, or others take advantage of her or fail to keep commitments
- Consistently does things she doesn't want to do because she is afraid to say, "No," she doesn't want to disappoint someone else, or no one else is taking care of it
- Fails to address problems until they are resolved for fear of "rocking the boat"
- Erupts emotionally in anger at others in her life instead of handling problems to avoid burnout, resentment, and fatigue
- Allows others to behave badly without saying anything, even if it is causing a problem
- "Walks on eggshells" to avoid upsetting people who have volatile personalities or anger issues
- When someone else is upset, she does everything she can to fix whatever is wrong
- Seldom asks for help herself, but is often helping others do things they could do themselves — so much so that these things become expected of her

So how'd you do?

Certainly these lists aren't all encompassing, but you're getting my drift as you see some strengths or opportunities. If you wish you were more of a King's daughter, please sign up for our free Strength & Dignity eCourse on my blog at www.NinaRoesner.com .

Can I just talk a minute more about this, please?

You need to know that if your husband doesn't behave in loving ways, if he is mostly harsh with you and your kids instead of being loving, if he is controlling and you are afraid of him, if you might be worried you could be in an abusive marriage and confused about how to handle it – *know you need to pair the Strength & Dignity element with respect or you will just reinforce what he is currently doing*.

We know God hates divorce but we also know that He calls us to live a life worthy of the Gospel. Maybe our husbands can treat us in a way that feels harsh and unloving, undignified. Maybe we respond in kind, convinced that this is the way we must stand our ground as women.

Maybe we see men as enemies of women in general and we feel obligated to fight a war against men on behalf of all women everywhere now and in the future.

The messages of the culture, psychology and even the church are swirling in our heads, filling us with confusion and ultimately fear, shame and despair. We have no idea what to do.

Our prayer is that God would still the chaos and His voice would be the loudest as He leads you through this process of learning how to respect yourself and your husband in a new way. We will learn specific tools to handle emotions, stress and conflict and implement boundaries in our marriages to keep them holy.

Just FYI, here are a few things you need to know before we begin:

1. *I'm assuming you aren't being battered. If you are being hit, pushed, held against your will, or if he is doing this to your children, please contact your local domestic violence folks. Those things go far beyond the scope of this course.*

2. I don't know if you have kids, **but verbal aggression in your home communicates to your kids that one person matters and the other (or others) don't.** These marriages are not about "oneness" and they don't bring glory to God or the church. A man who is harsh with his wife is not "living in an understanding way" nor is he treating her as an "equal heir" (1 Peter 3:7) nor is he loving her as Christ loves the church (Ephesians 5:25). When we respond in kind, we are dishonoring God as well.

3. **While what many Christian authors have written for Christian women dealing with verbal aggression is true, I've talked with a number of the authors of these materials and their success rate of turning a marriage around is less than 2%.** So without being respectful, kind, gentle, AND speaking the truth in love, and addressing his sin against you Matthew 18 – style, you may end up out of the hell you are living in, but your marriage is unlikely to be saved.

4. Lastly, **your self-esteem may be so tanked that you doubt yourself.** So that needs to be improved.

1 Peter 1:6 says, "So be truly glad. There is wonderful joy ahead, even though you must endure many trials for a little while."

Ugh. Trials. Really?

Take heart. The text goes on:

"These trials will show that your faith is genuine. It is being tested as fire tests and purifies gold ... So when your faith remains strong through many trials, it will bring you much praise and glory and honor on the day when Jesus Christ is revealed to the whole world."

No, it won't be easy. But it will be worth it.

Much of what we're going to address will be in learning how to have healthy, God-honoring boundaries.

Yes, I said, "BOUNDARIES." Doesn't that fly in the face of submission? No. We don't believe it does. We believe in BOTH. We think the Bible clearly says "both." We even believe Jesus did both.

Here's why "boundaries" are a topic of great importance:

By not having boundaries, or using them incorrectly, *we essentially destroy the opportunity for others to easily respect us.*

We make it harder for them to treat us well.

We make it easy for them to treat us like a doormat. Not that their behavior is okay, nor are we to blame for it, but *we can create an environment where respecting us is easier for others.*

People who *earn* our respect naturally set boundaries for themselves – that's ONE of the many factors that earns them respect in our book. They also often respect other people's boundaries – that's another respect earning action. Finally, they set "protection boundaries" for those who cannot protect themselves.

Chew on those three key elements of healthy relationships for a moment. Healthy people:

1. Set boundaries for themselves
2. Respect the boundaries of others
3. Set "protection boundaries" for children, the elderly, or those they lead

This looks like a number of things – for example, **Sarah might set a boundary for herself that she is not going to eat dessert on days she doesn't work out, and when she does eat dessert, she is going to keep it under 400 calories.** She might have a boundary where she stops a conversation (while communicating respectfully – ie: "I'm feeling attacked right now, so I am going to take a break from this conversation. We can finish it later when we are both calm.") instead of letting herself become emotional, because she knows she is capable of saying something to hurt someone else, or allowing herself to be discounted or diminished as a person by the behavior of another. She might respect her daughter's boundary of not wanting to be tickled when she says, "Stop!" She'll respect her husband's boundary of not discussing anything "heavy" right before bed because he knows he is not patient then.

Protection Boundary Caveat: These only apply to kids or the elderly. Sarah may set a protection boundary for her kids of a limited amount of "screen time" because she knows it diminishes their ability to focus. Due to the complex nature of parenting, we won't be discussing "protection boundaries" much. To get into them would be an entire parenting course, and that's not the context we're looking at and not all the women here have kids. We do need to mention it, because you will wonder about how boundaries fit with kids as you set boundaries for yourself. Sometimes, as moms, we'll establish a protection boundary in the middle of a conversation between siblings or with the children's father if disrespectful communication is occurring.

- **With siblings**, it might look like this: "Jake, I know you love your brother (respecting him and assigning good motives) and your behavior right now is crossing a line of respect. I'm stopping this conversation so both of you can cool off and you can talk about it later when calmer heads prevail."

- **With our husband,** (say your daughter has an idea and before she can even get it out, he's dismissing her, "Laura, I'm sensing you are feeling like you aren't being heard, is that right? I want to make sure we fully understand your idea before we discuss it. John, can I help a second? I think Laura would like to be validated by us before discussing what she wants to do with her hair. Do you mind if we hear her out before we discuss it further?"

I know when I was a young mom, I didn't seem to have any boundaries – I wore myself out, didn't ask for help, and in the long run, it effected everyone. Those "small" decisions I made that seemed loving at the time cost us all a lot. But you know what? Even though I wouldn't do things now the way I did them then, I'm still grateful for the experiences – God will use it all – so don't spend one single second on regret. You are here NOW because there is a season and a time for everything. This is "the Now" you are supposed to be in.

Something we need to really understand before we move forward too far is this: boundaries are something we do for ourselves to protect and to create joy while honoring God. **We also need to understand that boundaries are NOT:**

- parental, where we start acting like someone else's mother
- punishment, where we are "disciplining" someone else
- controlling, so we can get what we want

Boundaries are based in Biblical truths of healthy relationships. They are also not going to protect us or lead us to joy 100% of the time.

Boundaries are Biblical – Jesus Christ talked extensively about boundaries. He chose when to reveal Himself to Herod and others, He left an angry crowd, He rested when He was tired, and He pulled away from the masses to be alone with the Father. He made choices that were good for Him and followed God (creating and holding to His boundaries while obeying God) even when tempted by Satan! Notice Jesus' boundaries did NOT put Him on the throne. Ours should not, either. Nor should they be parental, inflict a punishment, or be controlling.

They should always be respectful.

Here's a few of Jesus' thoughts about boundaries:

- **Protecting Prayer Time:** "But when you pray, go into your room, close the door and pray to your Father, who is unseen" (Matthew 6:6).

- **Be Honest, Clear and Concise:** "Simply let your 'Yes' be 'Yes,' and your 'No,' 'No'; anything beyond this comes from the evil one" (Matthew 5:37).

- **Serve God First:** "No servant can serve two masters. Either he will hate the one and love the other, or he will be devoted to the one and despise the other" (Luke 16:13).

- **Please God, Not People:** "How can you believe if you accept praise from one another, yet make no effort to obtain the praise that comes from the only God?" (John 5:44), "But Peter and the apostles replied, "We must obey God rather than people." (Acts 5:29)

- **Obey God:** "Whoever has my commands and obeys them, he is the one who loves me. He who loves me will be loved by my Father, and I too will love him and show myself to him" (John 14:21).

- **God Sets Boundaries to Protect and Grow Us**: "Every branch in me that does not bear fruit he takes away, and every branch that does bear fruit he prunes, that it may bear more fruit." (John 15:2)

If you want more from your marriage and want to stop feeling like a doormat, please join us in the Strength & Dignity eCourse. It's free. <u>Here's where you sign up if you have 101 Ways as an eBook.</u> If you have this in print form, just go to my blog then to the "Wives" tab. The Strength & Dignity eCourse is under that one.

If you do it alongside the <u>Respect Dare</u> book, you'll also improve your marriage in a dramatic way. So more than protect yourself – birth JOY into your marriage by fully honoring and obeying God.

Regardless of where you're at in the Princess versus Peasant department, you'll need to be respectful, so we'll move forward now with understanding respect and why it matters so much to men. Please know I'm just doing the next thing that I sense God wants me to do. I'm just excited you want to work on your marriage. I am deeply motivated to help you do that in any way I can – although please be aware I'm not a theologian, psychiatrist, or professional counselor. I am a professional trainer – and we do get results from our training classes, which is why I get so excited about them. At any rate, let's get started by talking about why respect matters.

Your RESPECT for another means NOTHING if you don't respect yourself.

RESPECT DARE

Why Respect Him?

If you want a marriage filled with conflict, strife, argument, and angst ... one where the result is passivity, eventually apathy, and potential divorce ... embrace the notion of "standing up for your rights."

Yes, at risk of being called a traitor to my gender, labeled anachronistic and a "doormat," I'm telling you to lay that notion down.

And no, it's not because I'm a martyr, masochist, nor am I into demeaning myself and womankind in the name of "religion."

I'm also not a 1950's housewife who wraps her identity up in her husband's job, kids' endeavors, latest bread recipe, and whether or not my furniture shines enough to bear my reflection.

I am not speaking about the workplace, but please know that I spent over two decades in corporate America, as an administrative assistant, a human resources manager, and as a professional trainer. I've also waited tables, so I understand work from both a white and blue-collar perspective. And no, I was never discriminated against. In fact, in a company completely run by men, with God's help, I paved a new path for all of our female employees - and never once did I have to "stand up for my rights" by shoving my opinion down someone else's throat or threatening legal ramifications. Instead, I spoke the man's language of respect. I was in human resources, so I knew the compensation situation for my position and others. Discrimination did not occur in my world - instead, my employers rewarded me greatly. I am aware, however, that many other women have been discriminated against – I do believe that we teach others how to treat us.

I am also aware that the first and second waves of the feminist movement and equal rights legislation did much for the work place. What I am saying, however, is simply that when one is a respecter of self (especially when that is rooted in being a respecter of the Temple of the Holy Spirit, which those of us who follow Christ are), and makes it easy for others to pay them respect, we can sometimes avoid discrimination – and teach others how to treat us well. I'm not suggesting this is the norm, but I think it could be if more women (and men) learned how to be respectful PEOPLE. And even though I am speaking in this book about marriage, know these principles apply in nearly all relationships - and they are extremely important to most men. They are also important to women – we want to be respected, too. If we will respect ourselves and others, we will garner that more easily. In our discussions on Focus on the Family, and Family Life Today! we cover these topics in great detail.

So why am I telling women NOT to "stand up for their rights?"

Other than the fact that Christ Himself did not do this?

Because regardless of where you fall in the "faith" discussion, I know something you might not. I talk about the entire foundation of this in the book *12 Truths to Change Your Marriage*, but I will summarize briefly here.

Men's and women's brains are different – significantly so – and the difference affects the way we interact with each other. If you don't believe me, check with the internet. Look into the differences in men and women's health. Do the research. It may not be politically correct to say, but boys and girls really ARE different.

And those differences matter in the way we interact in relationships.

There's a shocking truth that is proven by biological, psychological, intellectual, and physiological research:

- Men are wired to compete and protect.
- Women are wired to connect.

These two simple yet complex truths provide much of the foundation for difficulties between the genders.

Inadvertently, we wives are setting off the "competition" and "defend my turf now!" responses in our men – by NOT learning to speak their language of respect.

And if we will instead become women of strength and dignity, women who encourage and bring life to our relationships instead of tearing them down with our own hands (or words), we can become women who truly *help* our husbands (and not from a "maid" perspective, but help relationally), women of influence, women who become part of the marriage equation, "1 + 1 + 1 = 1" (husband plus wife plus God = oneness) and represent Christ's relationship with the church, which is something beautiful. Notice there's nothing "doormat" in this suggestion.

Scientific research supports the Biblical instructions when it demonstrates that men and women's brains are significantly different from each other, resulting in differences in behavior, communication, and information processing. There have been a number of studies done and books written recently that in essence are meta-analysis of the available data. A list of them is available on the "Resources" tab on my blog, www.NinaRoesner.com. The studies are provocative, but the results stand clear. Granted, while there are exceptions and variances in degrees for both males and females, there are some important generalities.

Bear in mind, too, that the myth of "women say more words than men in a day," has been debunked. Some research even suggests that men speak more words than women do - most current research agrees, however, that men speak more in work environments and women speak more in relationship-based environments. Some research suggests that the volume of communication occurs where the gender is considered "expert" or of "higher status."

What remains true and provable is the physiological research demonstrating the differences in the real make-up of the brain itself between the genders. It is good to remember, however, that within the differences themselves, there are varying degrees. For example, while most research demonstrates men are "isolationary" (having few close relationships), there are men who are gregarious and have many friends. Recognizing what the overall tendency is can be helpful in helping people sort through what they are dealing with inside their own relationships. The other factor that needs to be considered - and should bring great hope to many wives is this: the research also demonstrates that experiences impact our development, regardless of gender. Both male and female brains can be altered by experiences. Social science is never an absolute and there is no intention on my part to injure or insult those who do not fit the "average" mold. Since I speak to large groups, I tend to try to "major in the majors and minor in the minors," paying most attention to the majority, while also giving attention to the minority. I like to say, "I like being average, most people are."

This little book's suggestions and the writings are based on the results of the research and show generalities. Please keep that in mind and try not to take offense if you or the guy you married are a little different. Know I don't "fit the mold" exactly, either, and neither does my husband. But we can learn much from the research, and it can help us navigate the murky waters of marital experience. Most scholars agree that because of the effects of certain hormones, the male mind is more equipped to interact with his world in a focused, practical, and systematic way – some research even suggests that men are more equipped to interact with objects, as opposed to people. The female mind is generally equipped to interact with her world with more empathy and relational emphasis.

In utero, as the boy's body begins to form, the hormones affect his brain structure. The connections between the right and left side of his brain referred to as the feeling and thinking sides, respectively, are severed, leaving him with a brain wired to be focused, but less in-tune with emotions of himself or others.

The average man's brain is structured for creating systems, being constantly aware of threats, and competing with others for dominance.

Stop a second.

Do you want your husband to feel threatened by you? Do you want him to feel like he has to defend himself against you?

What would him having that perception do for your relationship?

The majority of men do not want to compete with their wives. And while most men say they want competent women, they also want to be the hero, the problem solver, the rescuer, the knight in shining armor. In a day and age when the entertainment industry portrays men as lazy, foolish, overgrown children, know that the one who validates his existence is YOU. The absolute last person he wants is to have to defend himself against is you - he wants to honor, cherish, love, and protect you. The problem is, our culture has influenced both of us, and when we interact, things go awry. The sitcoms have modeled sarcasm and harsh startups as the ground rules of interaction and our snarky jabs at each other destroy any potential for love and respect to flourish mutually.

Do you think that arguing with him works better than respecting his opinion, being a good listener, then gently suggesting another thought to consider? Is this how YOU want to be treated?

Has constantly "standing up for your rights" been working anyway? Has the frequent defense for yourself brought you more intimacy and closeness?

I know it has not.

Perhaps you are fine with creating either an angry man, or a passive man. Know this is the outcome for many women who frequently practice, "standing up" as their way of getting their way.

Don't get me wrong – there are times to stand firm and communicate solidly, to calmly state your position unwaveringly. I'm not talking about those. If your attempts to resolve problems are ending in shouting matches, slamming doors, name-calling, harshly spoken words, or end in tears of anger, something needs to change in how you approach resolution – Christian or not, research shows that these type of behaviors often damage the marriage to the point that it is more likely to end in divorce.

For what it is worth, I'm also not talking about allowing yourself to be abused. That's a totally different situation.

Let's go back to your husband's brain - it is created for protecting his turf by defending it. Studies have shown that regardless of attempts to gender neutralize toys and environments, "boys will be boys," in that they engage in attempts for dominance in play. As men, they often exert intense effort to maintain and improve career standing. This competitive nature accounts for their overwhelming presence at the top of the heap in careers and the military. Right now, the executives at the highest levels in corporations are predominantly male. The majority of "dangerous" careers like police, firefighters, and the military are also men. This does not discount a woman's ability to do these jobs, but rather highlights a man's ability and natural desire to perform them. Back to the physiology, men are also low in the bonding hormone, oxytocin.

Conversely, the female brain maintains multiple connections between the thinking and feeling halves, resulting in a more holistic approach. She interacts with her world in a more empathetic and relationship-oriented way, understanding emotional cues better, and the relatedness between events. Women, on average, see better and hear better than men do – thereby picking up on non-verbal cues more easily. That's why he can look in the refrigerator sixteen times and not see the ketchup bottle – but because she sees the entire refrigerator, she knows it is right next to the salsa on the third shelf. We like to jokingly say it is because the uterus is really a tracking device, but the reality is, women actually have better holistic vision. Women also have more oxytocin, which creates emotional connection within a few minutes of interaction. Women also do not measure "success" the same way men do. They will give up status to spend time with their children as relationships are more important to them. Research also supports the lack of high percentages of women in corporate executive jobs due to this last fact, rather than attributing it to diminished abilities. Women, in general, value their relationships and families more than their careers.

Men, generally speaking, do not experience this in the same way. Men will, however, demonstrate their love for their families by working hard for them. That is not, however, to say that men are not interested in bonding with their families. Overall, men do take longer to connect, even with their own children - and bonding is linked to the amount of care they participate in. So if a woman wants her husband to bond with their baby, she needs to let him take care of the baby – in his own way.

Too often we hear stories of men who give up on learning how to care for their babies because their wives criticized their efforts – and as a result, they grow into men who are detached from their families. Without these important interactions, the eye contact, the touching, with his own children, this new dad will not (over time) begin to generate more oxytocin, that bonding hormone. Men, in general, even have fewer intimate adult relationships.

In terms of married affinity, men need physical touch several times a day to maintain oxytocin's bonding result, while women's need, while present, is less. In general, women connect and men compete. This is not to say that men do not connect and women do not compete, but rather their natural tendency is the opposite. For example, a woman would not naturally be wired to compete with her daughter for her husband's affection – she easily accepts and actually encourages their relationship because she is connected to both. Likewise, a man is not naturally going to start talking about personal things with someone he just met, but women can bond and begin sharing within just a few minutes of interaction.

There are also varying degrees of these differences within each gender, based on how the hormones (particularly testosterone) have washed the brain over the developmental years. This is why it is nearly futile for anyone to give you a prescriptive 100% accurate answer for what will absolutely work in your marriage. The truth is, your unique wiring combined with your husband's unique wiring make for a marriage cocktail that is unique to you. Some men have a more "female" brain, while some women have a more "male" brain. Women who have an inordinate amount of connections between the right and left sides of their brains and have a huge amount of estrogen and oxytocin may struggle with being concise and overly emotional. But if she has more testosterone and an average amount of connections, she will likely be more objective and struggle less with emotional control. Men who have extremely high amounts of testosterone washing in development and very little estrogen and oxytocin will be extremely analytical. The jokes about engineers and accountants exist because there is a bit of truth in them! :)

We also know that women are typically the ones who experience dissatisfaction first in their relationships with their husbands. They are usually the ones to instigate counseling or suggest books or seminars. This is in part due to the fact that they are more relational by nature than men, on average and are generally more aware earlier when something is awry in the relationship. Given that women are the first to begin sensing the problems exist, our goal is to equip them to be the ones to begin to solve them. Because of each gender's natural wiring, we suggest wives impact their relationship in ways which facilitate more satisfaction. The bottom line is that wives have a powerful opportunity to create an environment in their marriage that either facilitates team work and cohesion, or creates conflict and competition.

As a product of second-wave feminism, I personally spent nearly the first decade of my own marriage "fighting for my rights" with the man I married. Nearly destroying our relationship, my methods of "standing up for myself" (also known as defensiveness) made *him* feel defensive and disrespected. Being a practicing Christian, I ran across a Bible verse that at first angered me: Ephesians 5:33, "and the wife shall respect her husband." Another verse suggested I "submit" to my husband, and I had the same reaction. Having tried everything else, however, I implemented both, and a decade later, I can say that those two verses literally saved my marriage. Once I learned to speak my husband's language of respect, and learned Biblical submission, boiled down, basically captured the notion of, "don't be a contentious competitor to him," I communicated less argumentatively and became happier in my marriage.

And, no, I did not give up my voice or become a doormat. We did not avoid conflict, either, but rather worked together better through differences of opinion. Even though I had been respectful as a professional woman, somehow I missed that element in my marriage. I chose to start treating my husband as precious to God. I viewed myself in that same light. Knowing that like many men, he struggled with how to communicate his feelings for me, I began asking my husband to do specific things that made me feel loved and respected.

I actively chose to create an environment where I removed myself as a competitor or a threat to him.

So yes, at the risk of sounding anachronistic, subservient and a traitor to my feminine gender, I actually suggest to wives that they respect their husbands to improve their marriages. What most people fail to realize is that the give and take of a loving and respectful relationship is nurtured and created with a ton of effort. It does not just happen. One of the biggest issues women face as well is falling into the trap of "mothering," "enabling," or "rescuing," their husbands. That concept is one which occurs when the wife forgets or doesn't know how to treat herself as the Temple of the Holy Spirit, respecting herself and making it easier for her husband (thereby helping him) to be respectful towards her. We talk about this quite a bit at our workshops and in our classes. It's really too much information for a little book like this.

One thing remains certain, however, the concept of "applied respect" has changed my marriage. I now have a marriage where my husband and I both seek each other's advice, make decisions together, and are both happier. Neither of us is perfect, but our marriage is better because of the continued effort on both our parts.

And that, I believe, is as close to "happily ever after" as any married couple could hope for.

If you want to join us in a life-changing journey and learn what respect actually looks like in marriage subscribe to my blog, take Daughters of Sarah®, join us in Strength & Dignity, or do *The Respect Dare*. Hope to see you soon!

Love to you,

Everyone loves lists.

"Just give me a list of things I can do…" they tell me. So here it is. But understand, the hard work that comes with heart change and marital transformation really takes place when we work our way through *The Respect Dare* (Thomas Nelson Publishing, 2012).

Like I said earlier, please also understand that I'm not trying to sell my book, or Daughters of Sarah®, our eCourse, or anything else. I know in talking about those things, it might seem that way, and I am sorry if it does. It's not my intent to do that. In fact, I give this list away on my blog for free as a download. I also give away the companion info, *101 Ways to Love Your Wife* as a free list on my blog. Those two pages are, at this time of writing, our only two viral pages. I would think that if I was trying to make money off of you (and we run a non-profit, a 501 (C)3 tax exempt organization), well, it wouldn't make sense to give you our viral content info for free, would it?

Am I called to equip wives, however? Yes.

Can a list do that? You bet.

Will Daughters of Sarah®, *12 Truths to Change Your Marriage*, and *The Respect Dare* do that also? Yes. And most importantly, they do it in community and in a different way.

The bottom line is, if you have a hard marriage, you can't survive it or thrive in it by doing it alone – you need girlfriends.

So yes, by all means, here's your list, but consider linking arms with your girlfriends and do more…together. Even if it is just getting together once a week as you do the list together and talk through it – that's something! – but please please please do something with this list with friends. You need community, especially if you have a hard marriage.

We all do.

I want to humbly invite you to gather more free information by subscribing to our TIPS! articles. I invite you to personally dialogue with us on my blog, and sign up for the TIPS! articles at www.NinaRoesner.com as well. If you do that, you'll get a free download of this book – and you can email it to as many of your friends as you want to. You'll also get an email once a week of good information on marriage.

We walk the rough road of doing hard things in marriage and family…together. It's not quite the same as physically being together, but it is a place where you can learn more and give back to others who are just beginning the journey.

Can I humbly confess to you that I feel like God did all these things through me, and He designed all of our training courses and materials? (I'm not trying to add to the Bible, by the way) He is even responsible for creating our eCourse. When I started in 2005, I was 100% certain there was no way we could ever put our training method in any type of video or online format. **I was wrong**. And when God wants something, He can just make it happen. I'd never written a book before (training materials, sure, but not a book!). I feel like I'm just supposed to get it "out there" – and I am well aware that if I had said, "no," He would have found someone else to do so.

The Respect Dare was finished in less than a month, perhaps just 15-20 hours of actual writing time, and I've had many people talk about the discipleship aspect of it, and the deep spiritual experience of doing it in community. Daughters of Sarah® is like nothing else out there – and *The Respect Dare* experience (whether done on your own, in a small group with the videos and guide, or as part of our eCourse) is just a sliver of what God can do through these materials.

I'm not taking credit here, btw, and know I also don't want the responsibility, either. I'm telling you these things because I'm just an average girl like you – I'm a mom, a wife, I cook, clean, drive people around and I've never been to seminary, and I haven't attended Bible college. I'm just like you! I also know He has a plan for you as well. And the best thing about the book, the courses, all of it, is that they deepen your relationship with Him, discipleship-style.

I'm super aware that God had everything to do with the discipleship aspect of the book. If you want to watch a half hour interview I did with several pastors that talks about the importance of the concept of respect to the average man. You can search "Techology Nina Roesner" and you'll find it on YouTube.

I just can't stress enough that doing the book in a community of women, crying and praying and working hard together is what I believe God intended for us all.

I know this list and explanations may be of help, but if you want REAL and lasting CHANGE, join with your friends in doing the dares. Come talk with us on my blog. I'd love to interact with you! I'd love to have you with us on this hard journey.

And more importantly, **I believe God might be grooming YOU for leadership** – by being a Titus 2 woman, helping other women learn these things and impact other families. **So yes, I know you are just trying to impact your marriage right now, but there may be a bigger picture out there for you to consider.**

Your marriage might be hard right now because you might be in Titus 2 Leader Boot Camp. And I'd love to meet you in person at one!

Just think about it…

While we've watched God work miracles in many marriages as wives walk through *The Respect Dare* together, we don't claim to know everything. **And some of these things to do might not "work" with your husband.**

But know that God will work a Jesus-sized miracle in your heart through a discipleship experience. And respect won't simply be an action you do for a guy you really don't feel that way about, but rather, a love response to a God who loves the livin' daylights out of you, a God who is changing your heart, one trusting moment after another.

And one day, like thousands of other women, you will wake up and discover that your marriage is better, you feel loved, and you actually DO respect this guy you married – because **God will have matured you, and made you more like His Son. And most importantly, you'll feel closer to Him – even if your husband doesn't change at all.**

You'll be experiencing God's love on a whole new level, and that's a thing words just can't even explain. I don't know if you'll get there the first time you do this, or the fiftieth… but it will happen if you persevere. Please note this list is not meant to fix your relationship – especially if your husband is abusive.

We suggest taking this list, putting the numbers on your calendar, and then start going through them one at a time. It's not as effective as doing the book, but you should start thinking about things a little differently at the very least by the time you get through them! Be sure to join me online for support and encouragement as you begin this journey!

So without further ado, I present you with THE LIST…

101 Ways to Respect Your Husband

1

Refrain from interrupting him in conversation.
Research shows that men interrupt to take control
in conversation, while women do it to empathize.

2

Make eye contact while listening to him.

STOP ~~pns~~ you
phone down!
Focus on him not the
kids, when he is
talking.

3

Avoid rolling your eyes while speaking with him.
This communicates that you think his ideas are
stupid – he'll stop sharing what he thinks with you
if you keep responding this way.

4

Smile pleasantly while conversing with him.

5

When he is speaking, listen intently, trying to understand.

6

Appear approachable instead of judgmental while listening, asking questions to further your understanding, even if you think you might disagree.

7

Avoid pursing your lips and scowling while speaking to him.

8

Understand his point of view when you disagree, knowing that even though he may not be communicating emotionally, he might feel strongly about his thoughts.

9

Affirm his point of view, especially when you disagree.

10

Do something he likes to do with him.

11

Help him carve out time to spend with his friends.

12

Choose carefully whether or not the issue at hand is worthy of disagreement – the more you are disagreeable, the less he will ask you for input.

13

When a course of action is decided upon, support the decision enthusiastically instead of begrudgingly.

14

If you disagree with a position he holds, after understanding and affirming it ("If I understand you correctly, you are saying...I can see why you would say that because...") let him know you have another thought ("A concern I have about this is," or, "What I am wondering is," "What I'm struggling with is...")

15

Continue doing these things even when he disappoints you (otherwise you'll lose credibility with him).

16

Don't take it personally when he commits an oversight – his mind is probably on something else and he isn't focused or forgot.

17

Say, "Thank you!" when he does something for you, regardless of what it is – wise women are appreciative of all things. Anyone can be grateful for big things, a wise woman is grateful for the small also.

18

Say, "Thank you for going to work," or "Thank you for looking for work today," if he is doing either. Wise people thank others for doing the things they do daily, instead of taking them for granted.

19

When you ask for something say, "Would you please…" Wise people do not assume attitudes of entitlement, but rather understand the preciousness of others to God and treat others accordingly, instead of taking them for granted.

20

Don't argue with any act of generosity he displays, even if you think it is not necessary, or if it's for you and you don't think you need it. Accept his generosity.

21

Compliment him on acts of generosity, "You are so generous! Thank you for doing that."

22

Don't correct his efforts in diapering, feeding, or playing with the baby, unless there is a significant safety risk involved. He will parent differently than you do. That is okay. If he wants help, he will ask you for it.

23

Have emotional control when you bring up issues.

24

Understand that talking about issues when you are upset does not yield the best result for either of you. If you sense yourself getting upset, say, "I need to take a break for a bit." Then pray. If he's upset, say, "I'd like to break for a bit to pray because I sense I'm upsetting you."

25

Don't get frustrated with him when he doesn't express his feelings well. Most men's brains are not "relationally-wired" but rather focused on problem solving, threat, and system development.

26

Accept his feelings, and affirm him for sharing them, even if you don't agree with his position ("That sounds like it is a difficult thing for you…I appreciate your sharing this with me. How can I help?")

27

Don't talk about issues when he is tired, distracted, or hungry.

28

Don't assume he has a negative feeling, instead, tell him, "I'm sure you have a good reason for what you are saying, can you share with me what it is? I'm confused."

29

Don't ask questions beginning with the word, "Why?"
Research by Shaunti Feldhahn shows many men
perceive that word as a challenge.

30

Say, "Excuse me," when you are trying to get his
attention, or touch him and say his name. You may
not realize how focused he is on what he is doing
at the moment and think he is ignoring you
otherwise.

31

Don't just launch into conversation, say his name and
then ask if he has a few minutes to talk about
something. If you switch topics in the middle of a
conversation, let him know by saying something
like, "Switching gears, now, okay…?"

32

If he does not have time to talk now, ask him if later
would be better, or if he would please suggest a
time that works for him.

33

Introduce him to people at social gatherings, even if he's already met them, unless they are very good friends of yours whom he sees frequently. "David, I think you've met my friend, Sarah." This helps him feel more comfortable in social situations with you.

34

Apologize by saying, "I'm sorry I did XYZ. I feel terrible that I ABC and will try not to do it again."

35

Don't be disagreeable in the way you share a different opinion. Being overly emotional gets in the way of what you are saying – and demonstrates a lack of self-control on your part.

36

Actively agree with him frequently, saying, "You are right! That's a great insight." If you sense him becoming defensive, help him STOP by saying,

"I'm not disagreeing with you – and I don't want
to make you defensive."

37

Learn how your stuff from your childhood effects
your perceptions and continue to work through
those things to grow.

38

Contact him via email or text to let him know you are
praying for him – check to see if he has any
specific requests today.

39

Initiate intimacy.

40

Cultivate your own relationship with God.

41

Take care of yourself physically – get rest, exercise, and eat right. You are the temple of the Holy Spirit – and you'll live a longer, healthier life if you are mature and responsible in this area.

42

Find out what "domestic support" looks like to him and do the stuff that matters to him.

43

Smile and greet him when you first see him and when he comes home from work (or you do).

44

Let him finish his sentences without interrupting and without finishing them for him.

45

Ask him what he thinks about stuff that's important to you or the kids.

46

Stop what you are doing when he is talking and make eye contact with him, being a good listener by being interested in what he is saying.

47

Give him at least one compliment a day that builds him up – point out a character strength and say why it matters.

48

Be enthusiastic about intimacy, pursuing him… and yes, I know this one is on here more than once! (There's a reason for that – bet you know what it might be…)

49

Encourage him to spend time with his friends, and make it easy for him to do so.

50

Touch him when you are speaking to him.

51

Make him favorite meals regularly if you're responsible for some of the dinners.

52

Ask him for advice about things you are dealing with.

53

Do what he suggests. God will often lead your family through your husband, often whether he is a godly man or not. (Do not follow him into sin, however).

54

Ask him daily if there is something you can do for him that day. Then do it.

55

Help him de-tox from his day by providing a quiet, calm environment for him to come home to.

56

Try to work your schedule such that you can relax and freshen up a bit before you see him at the end of the day.

57

Get dressed daily and avoid "letting yourself go" physically.

58

Let him know daily something you admire about him.

59

Don't poison your marriage with criticism. Ask him for what you want, but refrain from telling him he is failing at something – it will demotivate him.

60

Ask him how his day went – then really listen to him about it. You need to know what's going on in his world.

61

If you break something of his, fix it.

62

Don't openly disagree with or correct him in front of others. If you must say something because the issue is of great importance, say something to him in private and do so by asking a question – "I am not sure I remember that the same way, babe. Didn't we XYZ? Or was that another time?"

63

When he apologizes, smile broadly, kiss him, and thank him for apologizing and understanding. Then tell him you forgive him. It's like it never happened.

64

Don't dredge up issues – if you choose not to confront him about something, you have chosen to let it go. You also have given him permission to do it again. If/When that occurs, deal with it, but don't keep a list of wrongs or bring up stuff from the past.

65

If he treats you badly consistently, it is okay to say to him, "I'm not feeling super-amorous tonight... you XYZ'd me today, and that's become a pattern because it's not the first time. I've asked you to stop, and I know you apologized, but it's starting to affect our relationship. I'm concerned that we're going to have major issues in this area if you don't keep your word. What are your thoughts?"

66

Avoid getting lazy in your relationship – ask God to keep your heart prioritizing your husband in your life.

67

When you see him, smile broadly, whether you have seen him 28 other times that day, or whether it is the first time.

68

When he comes back from work or an errand, stop what you are doing, and greet him enthusiastically. "Baby! I'm glad you are back! I missed you!" (So okay, you might not call him "baby"…)

69

Let him know how whatever he does positively impacts you. "Baby, thank you for consistently paying the bills for our family – I appreciate that and am thankful to not have to deal with that stressful task.

70

If he lets you know something is bothering him, be a good listener – don't give him advice unless he asks for it.

71

If you have an idea that might help him with something, come to him and say, "I've been thinking about how ABC has been bothering you, and this might be a silly idea, and you probably already thought of it, but would it work to XYZ?"

72

If he wants to talk to you and you are in the middle of something (texting, email, completing a sale, reading the last paragraph of a chapter, a complicated work project, whatever) don't try to multi-task. STOP. Say, "I really want to hear about this – I want to give you my undivided attention, and I'm in the middle of a conversation with so-and-so about such-and-such. If you give me just five minutes, I'll be all yours."

73

Better yet, if it is something that can wait, let it wait –
that way he'll feel important to you.

74

If he approaches you for sex at an inopportune time,
give him a passionate kiss and say, "I am SO into
this right now! And you know what? I'm dyin'
because I'm late to XYZ – so you keep this fire
burning until (time later that same day) and you
will be so very glad you started this…I don't know
how I'm going to think straight today now that my
mind is on YOU!" Wink.

75

If he gives you a gift, receive it graciously, no matter
what it is. He will grow more confident as a gift
giver over time and will most likely figure out
what you really want, unless you criticize the
desire to improve out of him.

76

If he doesn't hug you back when you hug him, ask,
"Can you wrap those muscular arms of yours all
the way around me? I love how safe I feel when
I'm enveloped in your arms." Then purr.

77

When he fails at something and tells you about it, no
matter how awful and dire the situation is, respond
with, "Honey, I am behind you. I believe in you.
You are a smart guy and a hard-working man and I
know we'll get through this." Then let him figure it
out. Pray for him while he does. Know he's
already kicking himself for failing at something, so
getting mad at him doesn't help and just makes
him demotivated.

78

Don't offer to rescue your husband or do something to
solve his problem. If he wants your help, he will
ask for it. He needs time to think through what to
do, and needs to know you trust him to figure it
out. If you mother him, you will turn him into a
dependent boy instead of allowing him to figure
out how to be a real man.

79

Don't make jokes at his expense especially sarcastic ones. Ever. Not in private, not in public. Not ever.

80

Don't demean him in public, especially sarcastically. Ever. If he didn't do something he said he would, speak to him as if he were a colleague of yours if you were in a fine educational institution. Do not berate him in private or in public.

81

Have grace if he makes a mistake or forgets something, even if it is important. Men do not think the same way we do – expecting him to act the way you (or another female) would is ridiculous.

82

Don't compete with your husband. If you must play against him, don't be out for blood. Try to set up game situations such that you and he are on the same team.

83

If you win at something and your husband loses, play yourself down, not up. No one appreciates arrogant attitudes.

84

If you lose at something and your husband wins, congratulate him on his skills – even if he behaves like an egomaniac.

85

If you are supposed to leave at a certain time, be ready to go at that time.

86

Use your husband's name when you are speaking to him, or some other appreciated term of endearment.

87

Follow up with him about a struggle he's shared about with you – ask him how it's going, especially if you sense it is going well, then look for an opportunity to compliment him.

88

Compliment him in front of his coworkers as often as possible.

89

Smile at him often around his coworkers. You communicate volumes to the people he works with by whether you admire him or not.

90

NEVER criticize him in front of people he works with or in front of your kids.

91

Talk about things he is interested in.

92

Engage in hobbies he enjoys with him.

93

If he is completing a task, just go hang out with him. Offer to bring him a glass of water or cup of coffee. If he asks why you are there, say, "I just like being with you." If he is like most men, he will appreciate your presence, even if you aren't working together.

94

If he is working outside, in the garage or something similar, ask if you can be with him while he does it.

95

Avoid arguing with him. Instead, try to find areas of common ground and talk about those.

96

Keep him up to speed and in the know with what's going on with the kids – don't let him get surprised.

97

Reserve emotional outbursts for your girlfriends. He doesn't know how to handle them.

98

If he asks where something is and it is right in front of him, just tell him where it is without pointing out that he should be able to see it.

99

Give him space to process conflict the way he needs to, even if that means putting space between the disagreement and the resolution.

100

Touch him in the middle of a disagreement. Better yet, plant a big kiss on him. It will help both of you.

101

Don't speak critically about his family, especially his mother. Handle conversations about his family with care, remembering that he loves these people.

102

Don't tell him directly that he is wrong, but rather after telling him, "I'm sure you have a good reason for thinking/doing ABC – do you mind if I ask you a few questions to help me understand? A concern I have is XYZ… how does that fit?"

103

(and yes, I know I said, "101," but the list kept growing…and I said "initiate" a few times…) The most important thing you can do for your husband is spend time with God, developing THAT relationship, as it is the most important one in your life.

104

Respect yourself.

This list is not intended to be everything you need to know to respect your husband, but it should get you off to a good start. Dr. John Gottman's research shows that couples who are happy have twenty positive interactions for every negative one. During conflict, they have five positive interactions for every negative one. Disastrous relationships have .8 positives for every negative — whether in the middle of conflict or not. Making positivity the normal environment in your home is the goal! If you want to impact both relationship with God and with your husband at the same time, do *The Respect Dare* book or take Daughters of Sarah® with some girlfriends. **It's the mission of our ministry to help you connect in healthy ways with God, yourself, and others.**

We would love to walk along side you while you learn about respect and continue on in your marriage journey. I hope to interact with you on **my blog** for all things respect!

Love to you,

Nina Roesner

Resources

The Respect Dare, Nina Roesner. Thomas Nelson (December 12, 2012)

12 Truths to Change Your Marriage: A Respect Dare Resource, Nina Roesner. Mentoras (August 14, 2015)

For Women Only, Shaunti Feldhahn.

The Surprising Secrets of Highly Happy Marriages: The Little Things That Make a Big Difference, by Shaunti Feldhahn. Multnomah Books (December 31, 2013)

Seven Principles for Making Marriage Work, John Gottman. Published by Harmony 1 edition (May 16, 2000)

http://www.webmd.com/balance/features/how-male-female-brains-differ

http://www.pnas.org/content/107/39/16988.abstract

Love and Respect, Emerson Eggerich. Thomas Nelson (2004)

Have a New Husband, Friday, Dr. Kevin Leman. Published by Revell (September 15, 2009)

Sacred Marriage, Gary Thomas. Zondervan; Reprint edition (February 4, 2002)

The Male Brain, Dr. Louann Brizendine. Harmony Publishing (January 25, 2011)

The Female Brain, Dr. Louann Brizendine. Harmony Publishing (August 7, 2007)

The Essential Difference, Simon Baron Cohen. Basic Books (August 18, 2004)

Made in the USA
Lexington, KY
05 October 2016